THE BELIEVER'S GUIDE

A Book of Discipleship

Yolanda Francine

Copyright July 2023 by Yolanda Francine

All rights are reserved. No part of this publication may be reproduced, scanned, or transmitted in any form without prior permission expressly written consent of author.

>Author may be contacted by emailing **TheBelieversGuide@yahoo.com**.

The Believer's Guide

DEDICATION

This book is dedicated to the new believer in Jesus Christ and also to those who have been on this road for a while and desire a closer walk with God. After you give yourself completely to Jesus Christ, you are now a new creature in Christ. You have been born again! Congratulations on your new life. You are a babe in Christ, a newborn. Even though you are physically a grown man or woman, spiritually you are a newborn. You have just turned your back on the ruler of the earthly realm to turn toward the creator of all. Just like a newborn does not know anything and must be taught everything, you are also learning so many new things you never knew before. I hope this book will greatly assist you in being watchful and careful as well as being steadfast and determined to see your new life, in Christ Jesus, through to the end. I am available if you need additional assistance with incorporating these principals into your daily life by offering a 10-week class to bring this book to life and sharing my personal experiences.

The Believer's Guide

Why I Wrote This Book

I am writing this book because there is progress in the process. This is the reason why I chose the picture of a road for the cover of this book. We are on a journey and from the beginning through to the very end, it is all a process of sanctification and understanding who God is and building a relationship with Him. Starting on this journey of learning of God and learning just who He is are two different things. One is superficial and the other is on a more intimate level. There are curves in the road that can surprise us and if we are not prepared, we can end up in a ditch. There are many pitfalls and pot holes on this road to heaven, but as long as we continue to hold God's hand, like a toddler holding the hand of the parent, our heavenly Father will guide us through safely. However, we must read and study the word of God in order to know who God is and to see and distinguish His moves and motives. Only when we seek God, will we find Him. Only when we spend time with God, will we communicate better with Him. Only when we take the time out of our busy day to put God first, will we hunger and thirst for His presence and long to become more like Jesus. By surrendering ourselves, mind, body, and soul to Him 100% we will become more than conquerors and live the abundant life that He promised us. This book is not only for those who just recently started their new life with Christ, but for all who seek a closer walk with God no matter how long you have been on this path. Don't just read this book, apply it to your daily life.

Your Page

Your Name: _____

Date of When you started this book: _____

This is your personal and private book, belonging only to you. As you grow in Christ, you will see a great change from who you used to be, to becoming a vessel of honor that God can use for His glory.

P.S.

Please keep your Bible with this book. You will need your Bible next to you as you read this book. Throughout this book, I have scriptures highlighted. Please stop reading and go look up the scriptures in your Bible. This will help you to:

1.) Learn the order of the books in the Bible,

2.) Know what the Bible says and,

3.) Give you a better understanding of what the Bible says.

TABLE OF CONTENTS

Dedication 3

Why I Wrote This Book 5

Your Page 7

Introduction   Self-Assessment 11

Chapter One - What You Should Be Aware Of.................13

Chapter Two - The Old You & The New You 16

Chapter Three - Faith Is The Key 22

Chapter Four - We Are At War! 25

Chapter Five - The Slippery Slope 28

Chapter Six - How To Prevent Slip Sliding Away 30

Chapter Seven - There Is No Third Choice 34

Chapter Eight - You Have A New Mission In Life 36

Chapter Nine - What Most People Do Not Understand 39

Chapter Ten - Are you a Lukewarmer? 41

Chapter Eleven   - Baptism, Communion, and Fasting 45

About The Author 49

Additional Information ....50 & 51

Self–Assessment

This book is for those of you who have just given your lives to Christ. Welcome to your new life! This is the book of do's, don'ts and warnings. This is the first book for you who have just gotten saved. It will have help in your early stages of growth in your faith in Jesus Christ. This book is also for those who have been saved for a while and want a closer walk with God. This will nurture you and warn you of pitfalls. These are not pitfalls that someone else told me about or that I read from someone else. These are all fresh because they are real and they all happened to me personally. I had to learn the hard way because I did not receive discipleship from my church.

Let's talk about what your life was like before you got saved/gave your life to Christ. What was your average day like? What types of things did you do? What type of people did you spend time with? What types of activities did you do with them? What was your mindset or what was your state of mind? What kind of attitude did you have? What was your behavior like? Please use the lines below to answer these questions.

_____
_____
_____
_____
_____
_____
_____
_____
_____
_____

_____
_____
_____
_____
_____
_____
_____
_____
_____
_____
_____
_____
_____
_____
_____
_____
_____

The reason why I want you to write these things down is to make them real. This is your personal book to write in. I want you to be honest with yourself. I want you to own who you really were, be transparent. You need to write down all that you used to be in order to see later how much God has changed or will change you. Do not sugar-coat it. Tell it like it was. Write the shameful, disgusting life you use to live and the wicked sinner you used to be. Write down the unbelievable things that you suffered and experienced. Believe me, when you pick up this book a year from now, it will shock you to see what you wrote here today. To realize that your life was such a wreck at one time, but is no longer that way because God has changed you and therefore your life has changed; this will open your eyes to the power of God.

Chapter One – What To Be Aware Of

The enemy wants to separate you from God. That's it. That is the goal. It is just that simple. The whole objective is to keep you from being 100% "all in" with Jesus Christ. That is satan's goal.

You may say that is a short paragraph, but it is just that simple. The goal of Satan is to stop you from being "All In". As long as you are 50% or 99% in with Jesus, the devil has you. Satan owns you if you are less than 100% "All In" for Christ. **Ephesians 4:27**. You may think, really? 99% is not enough? The answer is Nope. You must be 100%. I cannot reiterate this enough. Some people may think, well as long as I go to church every Sunday, then I will go to heaven. Nope. Some others may say, I give to the homeless, I do volunteer work and I don't curse, drink, smoke and I will give the shirt off my back – surely, that will grant me access to heaven. Nope. Granted, God wants us to help those less fortunate than ourselves, but that alone will not get you into heaven. Satan tricks people into thinking that being nice will get them into heaven. Thou shalt be nice is not the eleventh commandment. Don't get me wrong, all those things are good and yes, we should all to do them, but those good works alone will not get you into heaven. The Bible says in **Galatians 5:9** that "a little leven leventh the whole lump." A little bit of baking soda will make the entire loaf rise. If you have a barrel of oil and you put one drop of dye from an eye dropper in the oil, the entire barrel of oil is spoiled. It spreads and penetrates the entire barrel. It permeates throughout the entire amount of oil. If the devil just has you doing a little bit of sin, then that is all it takes to separate you from God. Wow! Some of you are saying, well what in the world does it take to secure eternity in heaven? I will tell you. It takes 100% submission to Jesus Christ. It takes your total devotion to God's will in your life. It takes your will and your way to be killed, so that you can live in Christ. This is called "the flesh dying daily." **Galatians 5:24-25, Colossians 3:5,** and **Romans 8:13.** You must discontinue living the way that you have been living all your life, and now start living in a new way. Instead of living your life, your way, now live your life the way God says to live your life. This is about total submission and total surrender.

Once you give your life to Jesus Christ, your life is in His hands. When Christ died on the cross for your sins, He redeemed you and now you no longer belong to satan, now you belong to Jesus Christ because He paid for your sins, so now you belong to Him. You are redeemed like a coupon and you were bought with Jesus precious blood. Your life belongs to God and if you give yourself over to Him to use for His glory, you will never regret it.

The things that you wrote down earlier, in your self-assessment, have got to go. Ask God to help you to discontinue doing those things, behaving in those ways, thinking those thoughts, saying those words, or hanging around those people. Although you may have been saved for many years, there is always room to grow. Sanctification is a life-long process, you are not perfect yet. None of us will be perfect until we get to heaven. But in the meantime, we all need to continue to work toward perfection in Christ. The Holy Spirit will help us to discontinue living in sin.

List these things that you must stop, write the details and be specific:

_____
_____
_____
_____
_____
_____
_____

The Holy Spirit will also help you to do the things you need to start doing, and behaving in the way you need to start behaving, and thinking the way you need to start thinking and saying the things you need to start saying and start hanging around those you should hang around. Let's list these things specifically. You may not know what they are yet, so I will help you with this part.

1.) Pray in the morning before starting your day. Maybe you go to work, work from home, or are an entrepreneur. Please set aside time in the morning to pray and ask God to lead you and guide you and help you to stay away from sin.

2.) Read your Bible daily. Find a Bible reading plan, or a Daily Bread, or Daily Devotion book, so that you can read a scripture and get an understanding to what that scripture means and how to apply that to your life today.

3.) Go to church and fellowship with other Christians. These are your sisters and brothers in the faith. They have given their lives to Christ and are seeking God daily, just like you.

List some other things that you need to start.

_____
_____
_____
_____

Chapter Two – The Old You and The New You

There is a huge difference between the old you and the new you. A whole lot of changing is about to take place and not all of it will feel good. A lot of the changes will feel bad, but don't worry, you are in God's hands.

Before you got saved, you were living for the devil and doing his bidding and committing sins, i.e., planting evil seeds. When bad things happened, it was because the devil was having fun at your expense. It was because you were sowing evil and then reaping the evil that you sowed. **Galatians 6:7-8.** The devil loves to make you miserable, that is how he enjoys himself. The worse your life gets, the happier he is. When we plant evil, that evil seed will grow and blossom into more evil. When you plant good seed, more good will blossom. Be careful what you plant, because everything you plant will blossom.

Instead of committing sins because the devil wanted you to, now you sow righteous seed to grow love and righteousness everywhere you go. Now that you belong to God, whenever you go through tests, trials and tribulations, it is all for your good in the end. You may wonder, what is a test, trial, or tribulation? It is when something bad happens. Now that you are no longer under satan's rule when these dark times come across your life, it is for several reasons such as: 1.) <u>Reaping what you have sown</u>. We have just discussed the type of seed you plant is the type of blossom or fruit will grow from it. Sometimes it takes a while before the blossom happens, whether it is a good or bad seed.

Can you think of an evil seed that you planted and the evil that blossomed from it? If so, describe it here.

_____
_____
_____
_____
_____
_____
_____
_____
_____

The other reasons why bad or unpleasant things happen is because God is doing one of the following: 2.) God is teaching you or 3.) God is molding you.

You will recognize when God is teaching you because you will have epiphanies. You will read something in the Bible and then something happens to bring God's word to your remembrance and you will say "Oh, that is what that scripture means." Sometimes, you will wonder why this or that happens and someone explains it and shares a scripture with you and then you will say "Oh, that's what that scripture means." When you learn these lessons, please take heed, write them down and remember them. Because if you forget the lessons that God teaches you, you will repeat that grade and it may not be pretty the next time.

Have you recently remembered a scripture that helped you through a difficult time? What scripture in the Bible reminds you of a lesson that God has taught you?

_____
_____
_____
_____
_____

3.) <u>God is molding you</u>.

When God is molding and shaping you, it is because He wants you to be the best person you can possibly be. Sometimes it may feel like chastisement. God is scrubbing away all the dirt of your past, cleansing you of all your unrighteousness. God is burning off all the old stains and melting you down and humbling you in order to make you pliable, which makes you easier to mold. He can't mold something that is hardened. He has to soften it before He can mold it. God is reshaping you into something brand new. God is molding the broken-down piece of pottery into a new masterpiece. You may say, "I am already the best I can be," well, not quite. You may be in good physical condition or have a great career or have a lot of money, but that is not you at your best. God knows better than you.

God is the potter and you are the clay. **Isaiah 64:8.** Have you ever seen a potter mold clay? He starts out with a shapeless lump. Then he starts to put it through different forms and stretching it out and pressing it inward. This lump was comfortable just being a lump, but now there are changes going on and that lump is being pressed and stretched. You can imagine these are uncomfortable changes for a lump. God is putting you in positions where you are forced to make a choice of allowing yourself to continue to be transformed by the renewing of your mind **Romans 12:2** or go back to the comfortable state of being the "old you" that you have left behind. When you realize that you are the lump of clay and that God is stretching and pulling and squeezing until He creates in you a new and beautiful masterpiece, just let go of your plans and surrender to God's plans. Remember, He knows better than you. Surrender to the masterful hands of God to do a work in you. **2nd Corinthians 5:17** and **Ephesians 2:10**. Have you experienced being molded by God? Do you remember how uncomfortable it was during that time? What old bad habit did He break in you? What new masterpiece has God shaped you into from that experience?

_____
_____
_____
_____
_____

God wants you to be the most Christ-like person you can be. It is being wise, strong, and bold all while shining your light for Christ no matter what your circumstances may be, during good times and bad. It is like either being an orange or a lemon. When we are squeezed by hard times, what comes out? Does sour lemon juice come out or does sweet orange juice come out? Either the sweetness of God's love or complaints, irritability, selfishness, and revenge will come out. Are you still praising God during hard and difficult times or are you complaining? **1ˢᵗ Thessalonians 5:16-18** Even if you are a nice person already, it is time to be righteous, holy and obedient to God; to do His will instead of your own. Submit yourself to His righteousness and not your own feeble ideal of righteousness. **Isaiah 64:6**. If you are weak, now is when God will make you strong, if you are shy, now God will give you Holy Boldness. **2ⁿᵈ Corinthians 12:9.** Your best is according to the word of God. Your best is yet to come. God gives all His children Holy Boldness to share the gospel. Have you had an experience in which you could have complained, but miraculously didn't?

_____
_____
_____
_____
_____
_____

This proves that God is changing you. This is something to rejoice about. When things don't go the way that you want them to go, or the way you think they should go, it is because God has a better plan. You can't see that because you are human and can only see what is in front of you. **Romans 8:28** says "And we know that all things work together for good to them that love God, to them who are the called according to his purpose." God sees the future and knows what is best for you and He guides your steps for your good in the future, even if you do not see it right now, God sees everything. **Jeremiah 29:11**

Have you had any of these experiences yet? Have you made plans or pursued goals, but things did not work out? Did things turn out even better because you did not achieve your earlier goals? Are you going through this experience now in your life? If so, write down what your plans or goals were. What did you want to achieve?

_____
_____
_____

Write down how the experience ended. Write down how you thought it would end, but now that God has brought you through it, how have things worked out in the end? How are things better now that you did not achieve your previous goals? How did God change your plans for the better?

Chapter Three - Faith is the key

Jesus Christ died on the cross. This is a fact. Historians of many cultures and nationalities can testify to this fact. Even other religious beliefs testify that this is a fact. But they have no clue as to why Jesus Christ was crucified. The Bible tells us why. Jesus was a sacrificial lamb. He took on all our sin. He took on the sins of everyone in the world. **2nd Corinthians 5:21.** How do we know if we are righteous? We know because God says so in **Romans 4:3 & 5**, and God is the one who declares us righteous, not us. **Isaiah 64:6** tells us that "our righteousness is as filthy rags." Things that we do and all our "good deeds" that we think make us "good people" does not get us into heaven. However, our faith in the Lord Jesus Christ is what God sees as righteousness. It is our faith that is counted as righteousness, not our works of obeying the commandments. **Genesis 15:6.** The reason why we obey God's commandment is to show God that we love Him, **John 14:15** and this is our reasonable service to obey God's commandments **Romans 12:1.**

Hebrews 11:6 You must have faith in this walk with God. It is a necessity! You can't be a Christian and not have any faith. You may have a little bit of faith and that is alright, because that little mustard seed of faith can grow and get stronger. **Luke 17:6** and **Mark 11:24.** Faith is a necessity when you pray. You may not be quite sure what faith is. Turn to **Hebrews 11:1** for the definition of faith.

Faith is a muscle, a spiritual muscle that you can't see. Think about a body builder and how big they are. They have huge legs and arms and can pick you up as if you were a toddler. How did they get that big? I will tell you. It is because they spent a lot of time in the gym lifting weights. Our faith grows just like muscles. The more we workout our faith, the stronger it becomes. The Bible says that we, Believers in Jesus Christ, all are given a certain measure of faith. **Romans 12:3.** You may look at others and think they have more faith than you, but that is only because they have been in the spiritual gym and working out their salvation in fear and trembling. **Philippians 2:12-13.** They have been in situations and had a little bit of faith and saw God come through and make a way out of no way. Then they had more tests, trials, and tribulations and used their faith again and saw God bring them through that storm and their faith got bigger. And because God brought them through those situations, they have faith that God will bring them through this one too. The more you use your faith, the bigger it grows. You must use it in order for it to grow. If you never face a mountain, you will never see a mountain move.

Write down some mountains you have faced. Let others share their mountains that God has moved in their lives. These are encouraging testimonies that glorify God and His power and wisdom in our lives. We need God. These are examples of when we needed Him most.

_____
_____
_____
_____

_____
_____
_____
_____

_____
_____
_____
_____

_____
_____
_____

Write down these triumphs so that you can remember what God did. Look back over these to remind yourself of how God brought you through. I will share something personal with you. I write down all my answered prayers just for this reason. I want to remember what God has done in my life and give Him thanks during my prayer time. My memory may fail me at times, but when I look back and wonder how I got over, it is when I read my answered prayers. In fact, every year for New Years Eve, me and my brothers and sisters in Christ come together to pray the old year out and to pray the new year in. We come together to share the major events that God has brought us through and give God thanks and praise. We testify to His power and we glorify Him. We share all that He brought us through in the last year and share our prayers for what we hope for in the new year. We all take turns praying for one another.

HINT: None of the 4 sections of lines above should be blank.

Chapter Four – We are at War

What is essential for those who have been a Christian for years and you newborn believers to know and realize, is that we are at war. I know this is news to you. This is bootcamp and I am here to prepare you for war. You may ask "Who is the enemy?" The enemy is the devil/satan. The enemy is the one who has had influence over you ever since you were born. The enemy is satan who has riddled your life with poor choices, which has landed you in dire straits. You may ask "Is the enemy really that bad that we have to be at war?" Well, little ones, to answer that question, let me ask you this: What was going on in your life prior to getting saved? Was everything "peachy keen"? Was everything "coming up roses"? What led you or drove you to seek a major change in your life? How has your life changed since you have surrendered your life to Christ? Answering those questions will give you the answer to how bad the devil really is and why we are at war with him.

Please stop at this point and go back to Pages 11 & 12

Take this time to go back to your Self-Assessment page and read it silently if you are in a group but out load if you are by yourself. Do that right now. Then come back and finish reading.

Because you were going through all of that and because your life was in that type of mess, this is why you are at war with the devil. Satan is the reason why you were in that mess in the first place. You should be angry that you had to endure all of that mess and it should strengthen your resolve to never go back to that life. You need to be determined to never let satan drag you back to that life again. Don't forget from whence God has brought you. When you forget where God saved you from, you start taking the precious blood of Jesus Christ for granted.

That "thing" that had taken you over and controlled you and drove you into misery with a terminal case of unhappiness and for some of you, even depression and anxiety. That is why you are at war with satan. **Psalm 51:5** says we were all born in sin and shaped in iniquity. This means we were all born as children of disobedience to the father of lies, which is satan. Ever since we were born, we lived in sin, therefore, for us, this was normal. This was all we had ever known our whole lives, so this was normal. We got used to it and accepted it as how it will always be. But before we jumped out of a window, we decided to give life one last chance to prove that this misery was not all there was to life and we came to God.

Beloved, your soul is at stake!!! Yes, this is war! You must protect yourself from the enemy because he is always and I do mean ALWAYS SEEKING TO GET YOU BACK into the state that your life was in previously. Satan has that "misery loves company" syndrome. He is going to hell and he wants you to go to hell too. Since he is going to burn forever, he wants you to burn forever too. The devil hates you! He really hates you! He hates you with a passion and wants you to suffer in drugs, alcohol, broken relationships, prison, depression, suicidal thoughts, whatever it takes to make your life a living hell and then die and go to hell and burn forever. Remember your Self-Assessment page? Satan is a stalker. He will never let up. Even after you have been saved for 50 years, he is still coming after you. He is relentless. He has tenacity that you would not believe. He will always be gunning for you and he will never stop trying to get you back. Satan is like the terminator; he never gives up on trying to demolish your life.

He is worse than a stalking ex from 2 years ago, still stalking. Satan, the evil one, he wants to bring all that pain and torture back into your life. Then you die, and then spend eternity in the burning lake of fire called hell. **1ˢᵗ Peter 5:8** and **Job 1:7**. This is what the devil wants for you. The devil is so slick, extremely skilled, and talented in stealing your joy. Satan is very experienced in trying to take you back to the hell that was your life. He has been doing this since he deceived Adam and Eve into disobeying God. That is a long time of experience. You may think he has no idea on how to temp you or trick you or set you up so smoothly, but you will not see it coming. Satan wants to drag you into a state of perpetual hell and then he will try to kill you physically so you will die in your sin and spend eternity in the lake of fire.

If this scares you, it should. Like I said before, this is bootcamp; spiritual bootcamp. I am trying to prepare you so that you do not fall into the traps I fell into. **John 10:10,** and **Luke 22:31**.

Please see the last pages at the end of this book for additional information regarding Spiritual Warfare.

Chapter Five – The Slippery Slope

This is when I began to stop being 100% "All In" with my Lord and Savior, Jesus Christ. Remember I said that just one drop of dye can spoil the entire barrel of oil? Yeah, that one drop; that little bit of baking soda that makes the entire loaf of bread rise. Yep, that little bit of sin did it for me. It did not seem like a big deal, but before I knew it, it became a VERY BIG DEAL. I hope you will learn from my mistake.

I will tell you what happened to me; for about a month, I started slacking in my Bible reading and my prayer life. It is called prayer life, because you should pray like your life depends on it, and it does, spiritually. You need to pray every day. Not only once, as many times as you can. Daniel in the Bible prayed 3 times a day. **Daniel 6:10**. That is not too much. There is no such thing as too much prayer. In fact, praying throughout the day would be great because this keeps us in tuned with God. Getting back to my mistake, I was busy with the new job, busy trying to get enough sleep to keep up with the new job, busy trying to catch the bus and be on time and the whole bus system had changed and I was busy trying to understand the new bus schedule so I would be on time for work and busy trying to make sure I ate breakfast so that I would not feel faint during the busy day at work. I was busy trying to write the first book for God, but I didn't do it because my laptop broke and I had no money to fix it and had to save up for 4 months before taking it to Best Buy for the Geek Squad to fix. I was busy trying to read my Bible and pray, but kept forgetting to do it. Really? Forgetting to read and pray, really? Really??? I was busy trying to do so many things that I was overwhelmed. One day of this and that lead to another day of this which lead to another day of this and before you know it, a week had gone by and another week had gone by and then a month. Then my whole world went bonkers! It was bananas! This is when I started acting out of character and becoming irritated and frustrated with everything and everyone around me. It did not dawn on me at first that I was feeling like I did before I got saved. Before I got saved, I used to always be "mad at the world" and now I am again "mad at the world," but I did not figure out why, until I fell on my knees asking God "What in the world is going on?" The Holy Spirit let me it was because I had strayed away from God. I was too busy for God. I was too busy being focused on other things to the point that these other things took priority in my life. God was no longer first in my life. Other things became more important. God went from 1st place, to 2nd place, to 5th, place to 10th place in my life. God wants to be in the top spot. Please do not make this mistake in your walk with God. Some have done this and have never recovered. They keep God in 2nd place, 5th place or 10th place. When we do that, we can never be what God wants us to be. He can't use us for His glory because we are hardened and remember, He can't use us if we are not pliable and easy to mold. We will not be the masterpiece that He sees in us. We can never reach that great potential that God has for us, all because we did not keep Him first. This means we have left our first love. **Revelation 2:4-5.** You better believe when The Holy Spirit told me what I did wrong, I repented for that sin. But suffice it to say, that I did not let that happen to me again. No more neglecting to pray and read my Bible. Please learn from my mistake. Do not let the devil take you away from God, do not go back into sin. **Galatians 5:1** "Stand fast therefore, in the liberty wherewith Christ hath made us free, and be not entangled again with the yoke of bondage."

Chapter Six – How To Prevent Slip Sliding Away

In other words, how to prevent this from happening in the first place.

In the Old Testament of the Bible, the hard pounding recurring theme is that God requires communication in His relationships. He requires prayer, Bible reading and praise.

1.) Prayer, is you talking to God and seeking God to speak to you.

2.) Bible reading, is God speaking to you through His Word.

3.) Praise, is you worshipping our heavenly Father and opening the communication up between you and God. Praise is when you are showing Him how much you love Him and desperately need Him and He will come close to you and you will be able to feel His presence. It is in that moment He will speak to you in some unique way.

Communication is an important part of any relationship, so it is with God as well.

Don't you require communication in your relationships too? You would not want the person you are in love with to only speak to you once a week, would you? You would lose your mind if the love of your life ignored you and spoke to you for only one hour per week. So, what makes you think that you should only pray and read your Bible at church on Sundays and then you're done? Don't you realize that God loves you and that is why God gave His only son to be sacrificed, in order to wash you clean with the precious blood of Jesus? **John 3:16.** Remember I said when you forget where God has brought you from, you begin to take the blood of Jesus for granted? Please don't take the precious blood of Jesus Christ for granted. You should be in love with Him too. Jesus is so in love with you that He willingly suffered almost 24 hours of torture, allowing Himself to be hung on a cross for several hours to be the sacrifice for your sin. Because He loves you, Jesus created a way for you to escape hell. Jesus took on the punishment for your sin, so that you did not have to go to hell to pay for your own sin by burning in the lake of fire for eternity. **2nd Corinthians 5:21.** Jesus loves you just that much. Don't you think you owe Him more than just one hour per week? I am writing this with tears in my eyes, beloved, please don't take Jesus for granted. Those who choose to continue living a life of sin and rejecting Jesus Christ will pay for their sins, eternally. But because we have put our trust in Jesus, we no longer have to pay for our sin. He paid it all and He went through all of that for us so that we would not have to burn for eternity. I am so glad that I put my faith in Jesus Christ instead of paying for my sins by burning in hell for eternity.

Our relationship with our heavenly Father and His son Jesus Christ and The Holy Spirit is so important and such a huge part of our lives. In fact, it IS the most important part of our lives. If you don't understand that last sentence, it is okay, you soon will. If you are just flat out defiantly disagreeing with that sentence, then you really don't understand the relationship between you and God.

Always stay in the Bible everyday. Always stay in prayer everyday. Never, ever, ever, get too busy. Never let yourself get distracted. We can easily become distracted by the phone. It can ding or ring to interrupt our prayer and then we never get back to prayer. A cute face can have us thinking more about them, than God. We can just get busy with life. This means you need to practice time management and be a better manager of your time. Now that you are reading and praying, you need to make sure you are diligent every day. It should be easy since you have given up the bad habits and bad friends. You should have extra time on your hands now. There are only 24 hours in a day. You need to work. You need to sleep. You need to read your Bible and Pray. Do not get too busy on the phone, surfing the web, hanging out, etc. Do not give the minor things in your life high priority. Living your life following Jesus now is your priority. Do not get tired of doing the right thing. **Galatians 6:9**.

Since you no longer do those sinful things, you have time on your hands. I will help you with building your new schedule of new things you will do, since you stopped the old things.

1.) Go to bed earlier so you can get up earlier to spend time in prayer and read the Bible and have your time of devotion with our heavenly Father. Stop staying up late watching tv. Go to bed early, so you can still get your proper rest and be refreshed in the morning to spend time with the Lord.

2.) Instead of surfing the net, spend time praying and giving God thanks for getting you through the day. Ask God to forgive for whatever you thought, did, or said wrong today and ask God to help you do better tomorrow.

3.) Forgive those who have done you wrong today. Whether it was the person who cut you off in traffic or your co-worker or boss, or something someone in church said to you. Forgive them. They are not perfect and neither are you. Remember and practice the scripture of **Mark 11:25-26**. If you do not follow this scripture, it will affect your prayer life.

4.) Attending church every Sunday and weekday for Bible study or small group.

5.) Witnessing with other church members. Sharing the gospel of Jesus Christ. You can also do it alone. Share with your co-workers or classmates. Share with others no matter where you are: laundromat, check out line at the store, bank, dry cleaners, deli counter, while picking your produce in the grocery store or even at the gas station, or while waiting at the bus stop.

Feel free to write down other new and godly things you are starting to incorporate in your daily or weekly schedule.

_____
_____
_____
_____
_____
_____
_____
_____
_____
_____
_____
_____
_____
_____

Chapter Seven - There is no third choice

There are only two choices: God or Satan

Maybe you did not know this because no one told you, so let me break this truth to you gently. You are human. There are two spiritualities. You WILL serve one of them. You get to choose which one you want to serve. Remember, there is no third choice.

Which one do you choose to serve? Which one do you choose to be your father? You were born, as a child of disobedience. **Ephesians 2:1-3** and **Colossians 3:6.** You were born in sin **Psalm 51:5** and satan was your spiritual father. **John 8:44.** You were on auto-pilot in serving satan. If you don't believe me, think about this. Have you noticed that a baby of less than a year old has tantrums and can make their body stiff because of their out-of-control anger? Have you seen a toddler, who can barely walk, go to the cookie jar that you explicitly told him not to touch, and he will steal a cookie as soon as you turn your back, then he will look you in the eye and lie to your face and tell you he did not do it, all while chewing on the cookie that is in his hand? I have seen it and I wonder, who taught him how to be disobedient? Who taught him how to steal? Who taught him how to lie? His spiritual father taught him, that's who! You may laugh and think it is cute, but that is because you think that it is normal. You think it is normal because this is all you have ever known since you were born, so it seems normal to you. Being born in sin is normal for a sinner.

Because Jesus had shed his blood, this gives you the opportunity to open your heart and accept Jesus Christ into your life and turn away from your old father in order to submit yourself to God becoming your new Father. **Matthew 6:24** states "No man can serve two masters: for either he will hate one, and love the other; or else he will hold to the one, and despise the other." You cannot serve both. There are only TWO choices. So, when someone says they choose neither, what they are really saying is that they refuse to accept Jesus Christ as their personal Lord and Savior and they want to continue to serve the devil. Because we are already born in sin and shaped in iniquity, we are already born serving the devil from the very start. Make a choice. Like I said, you WILL serve one of them. You will be a servant period. You only get to choose who you want to serve. You only have the freedom to choose which one, not the freedom whether or not you will serve.

Joshua and Elijah would have something to say about this. **Joshua 24:15** and **1st Kings 18:17-29**. Please stop now and take the time to read what they said about the matter. You will see that God felt a certain way about it back then, and God feels the same way about it now. God never changes.

Chapter Eight – Your Mission as a Christian

Now that you have a new life in Christ, your life has changed. I know you have many questions, so let's answer some of them. **1.)** What is my mission as a Christian or follower of Jesus Christ? What is my job? In other words, "What am I supposed to do now that I am a Christian?" Just so you will know, a Christian is someone who follows the teachings of Christ. **2.)** Why should I tell people? **3.)** What if I am shy? **4.)** How do I tell them? What approach should I take? Let's get started.

1.) What is my mission? Your mission is to share the gospel with others. Jesus not only told us, but He commanded us to do this in these scriptures: **Matthew 28:18-20, Luke 24:47, Mark 16:15-16, Acts 5:42.** A commandment is NOT an option, but a "must do." If you are like me when I first got saved, I did not know what the gospel was. The gospel is **John 3:16**. God sent Jesus to die on the cross for our sins. Jesus was the sacrificial lamb whose blood atoned for our sins. Jesus died, but God raised Him from the dead in 3 days. Jesus walked around and continued to teach for 40 days with the disciples after He was resurrected. Over 500 people are witnesses to the fact that Jesus was resurrected, then Jesus ascended into heaven and is sitting on the right-hand throne of God. First pray and ask God to help you understand it, then go read it. If you still don't quite get it, I understand. It took time before I could put it into words. You can always share your testimony, i.e., your personal story of how you came to Christ and how He has changed your life. This is perfect. The more you do it, the better you get. It will become a natural part of you in no time.

2.) You may say why should I tell everyone I know, that I am following Christ? Believe me, it is always easier to do it when you first get saved because you have just recently chosen not to hang around your old friends to do the same old things you used to do. This is your way of breaking ties with them immediately. This is how you break free from the yoke of sin. As a follower of Christ, you should no longer spend time with them anyway, because spending time with them will tempt you to go back to doing those things that you used to do. For Example: if you and your friends were mud wrestling and then you got up and went to take a long hot shower. Why would you get back in the mud again? You need to tell them why you are no longer going to hang out at the bar, why you are no longer going to do drugs, why you are no longer going to curse like a sailor anymore. They will wonder why, so get it out into the open. Tell them as soon as possible. There is no need to put it off. They will listen, because they are wondering why you have changed and this is your opportunity to tell them. They want to know anyway, so you might as well tell them.

3.) You may say you are shy. Let me ask you a question. If you saw a great movie or heard a fantastic song, would you share that with your friends? Of course, you would. Would you keep it a secret? No, why would you? Have you ever shared any information with your friends? Of course, you have. You would share that great movie or fantastic song with them. Why? Because they are your friends and you want to share the good news with them. So, go ahead and share the good news of Jesus Christ with them. **Matthew 10:32**. They will only have two responses: "no thank you" or "yes, please tell me more." If they are not interested, you tell them that you have decided to follow Jesus and that leads you in another direction. **Matthew 7:13-14.** You are now on a different road going in a different direction. Now is the time to say your goodbyes. **2nd Corinthians 6:17** and. However, if they are interested in learning more, bring them to your church. Either you agree with **Romans 1:16**, or you are ashamed of the gospel. Jesus will deny you just like you will deny a stranger who asks to come into your home. Jesus has something to say about those who deny Him. **Matthew 10:33-38** and **Mark 12:30-31**. Remember, God wants to be in 1st place in your life. He will not take a back seat to other things, other people, or yourself. God will not settle for 2nd place.

4.) You may ask "How should I approach the subject?" Since you need to tell them that you will no longer drink, smoke, lie, steal, use profanity, take drugs, watch porn, rob banks or whatever you all did together, they will ask why not. You tell them that you have accepted Jesus as your Lord and Savior. Tell them how you have peace now. **Philippians 4:6-8.** Tell them how you no longer feel lonely or depressed. If you feel you would be in danger if you saw that certain person from your past again, then please be safe. It may be safer to just stay away from certain "old acquaintances."

Chapter Nine - What People Don't Understand

What you are not understanding; is that this is a whole new life, not just a side bar. This is not just something to do on Sundays. This is not about being traditional. This is not about impressing anyone. This is not about being accepted by "the good people" and looking like a "good person" or playing the role of one. No, that is not it. Please understand, this is a Whole New Life. You Are A Whole New and Different Person With A Whole New and Different Life.

You are no longer the person you once were. **Philippians 1:6.** You are no longer interested in behaving in the way you once did. For example: Before you got saved, you would gossip about others and talk badly about others behind their back, or you would curse someone out for stepping on your shoe, now you don't. It no longer occurs to you to curse someone out anymore. If you are still gossiping and back-stabbing others and cursing people out for stepping on your shoe, please pray and ask God to clean your heart. **Matthew 15:11** and **Psalm 51:10-12.** Now when someone steps on your shoe, you instantly forgive them. That is a big difference. Before you got saved, you used to discuss sexually lude acts or say negative and degrading things about others, now you would rather discuss the Bible and encourage others. Now you want to talk about Jesus. **Philippians 4:8-9.** God's peace fills your mind and heart with peace and love and you handle things differently. You see things differently which enables you to experience them differently and react to them differently.

Now you pray and read your Bible and spend time sharing the goodness of God with others who want to hear about it. This is what I mean by your entire life changing

It is all or nothing at all. This is not a little thing; it is your entire life changing. Now your life revolves around Jesus Christ. Everything is all about Jesus. You must get this. You must understand and accept this. Are you ready for a completely new life, or are you a lukewarmer?

Chapter Ten – Are You Really Saved or A Lukewarmer

You may ask, "What is a lukewarmer?" Let me give you the definition. A lukewarmer is a person who is a sinner, but hangs out in church, acting like the people in church, but does not have a relationship with Jesus and is not saved. **2nd Timothy 3:1-7.** The church is full of these kinds of people who make excuses because they want to disobey God's word. A lukewarmer is a sinner going to hell, but spends some time in church for an hour on Sunday morning and may even show up at Bible studies to keep up their image, but for the rest of the week, they are living a sinful life. They have the form of godliness, but deny the power thereof. **2nd Timothy 3:5.** This person may fool some people in the church, but they are not fooling God. He knows they are a sinner on their way to hell. If this, is you, why are you trying to impress people? Why not be honest with yourself? Make a choice. Either serve God or continue serving the devil. Either way, be 100% and stop faking.

Some people may ask: "How do you know if you are saved?" This is a very good question. You are very smart to ask this question and it is very important to know the answer. Your very eternal soul depends on it and it is crucial to know the answer. I have asked this question myself. The reason why I asked is because I was brought up in the church as a child. I spent my life in church until college. When I was a child and teen, I thought I was saved because I went to church and Bible studies. But now I realize that I wasn't saved back then. This is how to tell the difference. There are a few differences: 1.) When I was a child and teen, none of my prayers were answered. **John 9:31.** 2.) When I was a child and teen my mind was not renewed and I was not transformed then. There was absolutely no change in my life, in my heart or my mind. **Romans 12:2**. I was not a new creature. **2nd Corinthians 5:17**. I was still the same young person doing undercover mischief as a teenager. I did not feel any different. 3.) I did not feel the presence of The Holy Spirit. There was no change in me. I did not suddenly enjoy church or enjoy Bible study, it was just a tradition, it meant nothing to me. I was still spiritually dead.

However, the reasons why I now know for a fact that I am saved are: 1.) I am a totally different person. God transformed me from the inside out and renewed my mind. I used to be angry, irritated, stressed out, frustrated and seriously unhappy. I was mad at the world and cursing everyone out. Now I am no longer like that. I just no longer have the desire to do those things anymore. I no longer have those feelings. 2.) My prayers are all answered. God answers the prayers of His children. **John 14:13-14**. It feels so good to see all of my prayers answered. God has 3 answers: Yes, No, and Not Now. The answer will be "no" if your request does not glorify the Father or is not in your best interest. 3.) My desires have changed. I want to please my Lord and Savior. I now have The Holy Spirit. **John 14:15-18**. I get excited when I tell people about Jesus, my King, and how He changed my life. I love to read and study the Bible and pray and talk about Jesus. I love to talk about Jesus and tell people about Jesus everywhere I go. I no longer have the old desires. 4.) My life has changed. My life is no longer swirling down the toilet like it used to. Now I have a future that God gave me. **Jeremiah 29:11** Wow, what a difference!

You may say that we are all God's children. You hear that all the time, however, that is wrong and a lie. We are all His creations, but only the saved or believers in Jesus Christ are His children. **1st John 3:1, John 1:12,** and **James 5:16** "…says that only the effectual fervent prayers of a righteous man avails much." And **John 9:31** says Now we know that God heareth not the sinner…" This all means that God does not hear nor answer the prayers of sinners. Only when a sinner repents of their sins and asks for forgiveness of sin, can they be forgiven and their prayers heard. Please do not confuse that with blessings. God sends blessings to the saved and unsaved. **Matthew 5:43-48.** We must be washed in the Blood of Jesus before God hears and answer our prayers. In conclusion, if your prayers don't get answered it is because you are not saved. You will never get your prayers answered until you surrender your life to God, only then will you belong to Him. Then you will have access to the promises that He gives His children.

God says in His Word for us to live a holy and sanctified life. Holy and sanctified means "separate." **2nd Corinthians 6:17.** This means we are to live separately from what everyone else is doing. If all your friends, drink, smoke and do drugs, you are to separate yourself from them and those activities. It is not only possible to live a holy and sanctified life, but very possible and very necessary. If it were not possible for us to live this way, then God would not expect it of us and therefore would not have commanded it of us. God created us and knows all our strengths and weaknesses. Therefore, He would not make the "mistake" of asking something of us that would be impossible for us to do. **1st Peter 1:15-16** says "But as he which hast called ye holy is holy, so be ye holy in all manner of conversation; because it is written, be ye holy as I am holy". It really gets my goat when lukewarmers say "It does not take all of that" "We don't have to do all of that" "God does not expect that of us because we are mere humans and are weak in the flesh and therefore are incapable of doing that and besides, it does not take all of that." Yes, It Does Take All Of That. This is exactly why Jesus spoke on this very thing in **Matthew 7:13-23.** He said in **Matthew 7:22-23** "……many will say to me in that day, Lord, Lord, have we not prophesied in thy name? and in thy name have we cast out demons? and in thy name done many wonderful works? And then will I profess unto them, I never knew you; depart from me, ye workers of iniquity." Then they will be cast into the lake of fire. These people who "claim" to be men and women of God will look you in the eye and say "It does not take all of that" will be the very same people who Jesus will say "I know ye not, ye workers of iniquity." Because the lukewarmers did not think it "took all of that" they will finally realize that yes, it did take all of that.

Chapter Eleven

Here are a few subjects of which new believers have questions.

Baptism

A true baptism is when you are completely submerged underneath the water. A sprinkling is not a baptism. When you are baptized this symbolizes that the "old you" is now spiritually dead and being buried as Christ was buried. When a person is dead and buried, you do not sprinkle a hand full of dirt on top of them and say they are buried. You completely cover them with dirt. They are totally underneath the dirt. Then when you rise out of the water, it is the "new you" who is now spiritually alive and you have now risen with Christ as He rose from the dead. You have risen from being spiritually dead and now are spiritually alive in Christ. **Ephesians 2:5.**

Fasting

The definition of Fasting is when you voluntarily refuse to eat. Some do it for health reasons. But here in this book we are talking about spiritual reasons. We, as Believers, will voluntarily Fast in order to breakthrough a spiritual hinderance or to grow to another level of closeness to God. While we are not eating, it is also very important to stay in prayer and reading God's word. In order to grow spiritually or to break through a stronghold in our life, we must Fast. A stronghold is when something has a hold on you like a particular sin that is hard for you to resist. You must let it go in order to grow in Christ and grow closer to God. **Mark 9:14-29.** Somethings will only respond to Fasting and prayer.

Communion

Some people call it the last supper, some call it communion. Either way, it is ceremonious. It is how we remember that Jesus died for us, by being the sacrifice for our sins. He took the punishment for us. Communion is how Jesus said that He wants us to honor Him for what He did for us. **1st Corinthians 11:26.** The Bible says that when we take communion, this is how we show Jesus that we are remembering Him and what He did on the cross for us. **Luke 22:19-20.** Even though we may give thanks to Jesus every single day for His sacrifice, taking communion, is the way that Jesus prefers us to remember what He did. However, we must examine ourselves to make sure we do not have any unconfessed sins. **1st Corinthians 11:28-32.** This is why I suggest asking God for forgiveness prior to taking communion to make sure our slate is clean before taking communion. **1st Corinthians 11:23-34.** Jesus was the sacrificial lamb or sometimes thought of as the scapegoat.

Let me explain the sacrificial lamb. In the Old Testament, God required the Jews to atone for their sins by sacrificing an animal. The animal was the substitute for the people, because technically, they were supposed to die for their sins. Even today sinners who reject Jesus as their savior will pay for their sins by burning in the lake of fire forever. We are all born in sin and because of our sins, we are judged and sentence to hell to be tormented forever for our sins and our rejection of Jesus.

Let me explain the scapegoat. Sometimes, the Jews would take a goat, and put their hand on its head to ceremoniously put their sins on the goat and then let the goat wonder around in the desert to die. **Leviticus 16:20-22.** Have you ever heard of the "scapegoat?" This is when someone blames you for something someone else did. Have you ever been the scapegoat? When you were a child, did you get punished for what your sibling did? Did the teacher blame you when it was someone else who threw the spit ball? Well, that is what Jesus did. Jesus was sinless, but yet He took on all of our sin as if He committed those sins and He was punished for it. **2nd Corinthians 5:21**

Jesus did all of this for us because He loves us so much, the least we can do is dedicate and devote our lives in service to Him.

The Believer's Guide

ABOUT THE AUTHOR

I am a dedicated and committed follower of Jesus Christ. When I first gave my life to Christ, it changed me and I have never been the same. I am still growing in Christ, as we all should, continuously. I have been witnessing for the Lord since 2016. I have been discipling women since 2018. I have also been teaching a free class on the Book of Revelation for women since 2020. God laid it on my heart to write this book and to share what I have learned through my experiences and mistakes. I did not receive discipleship when I first got saved. I met so many who are in the same boat. This is precisely why I am writing this book. I remember the day I gave my life to Christ; I asked the following questions: How do I pray? How do I read the Bible? I did not receive assistance with either of those simple, fundamental questions. It takes longer and is more painful to learn on your own, how to grow in Christ without discipleship. But if someone would have warned you ahead of time, it would have saved you a bad experience. We are in the last days and time is short, so discipleship is most necessary now. Therefore, I wrote this book, to help you skip the pitfalls, as well as, learn, apply, and practice growing closer to Christ in your daily journey. Growing in Christ is how we receive the abundant life that Jesus promised us. This book can be used by an individual, taught in a small group, Bible Study or Sunday School Class, as well as, attending my coaching class. Please see more details on the next page.

Yolanda Francine

Additional Information

I want to give you my personal thanks for reading this book in seeking a closer walk with Jesus Christ. I commend each of you for taking your relationship with Jesus seriously. My personal thanks to churches and other organizations for purchasing this book for each member of your small group, Bible Study or Sunday School class. If this book has been helpful to you in your walk with Christ, please share your experience with others and recommend this book to them so that they can grow just as you have. If you want to share your thoughts on the book, please feel free to share your message on **Twitter** under the name **New Believers Guide.** I have a **Professional Profile** on **Twitter**. My Twitter handle is **@New_Believer_G1.** You can also find me on Twitter under the **Category: Religious Book Store.** Please let me know how this book has given you new information that you did not know, or has given you a better understanding of concepts that are familiar to you.

I want to offer you the option of attending my coaching class on the principals of this book. Whether you are an individual, Pastor, Chaplin, church, or an organization, please contact me if you are interested in the ten-week coaching class that corresponds with this book. Please email me directly at: **TheBelieversGuide@yahoo.com.**

The Believer's Guide A Book of Discipleship can be purchased on **Amazon** and their international distributors.

Also, look for new books coming out before the end of this summer of 2023. There are two upcoming books in The Believer's Guide series. They are the following:

As we grow in our spiritual walk with God, we are to bare fruit. You may ask "What kind of fruit?" Well, I will explain it all in the upcoming book: **The Nine Fruits of the Spirit – Are you growing fruit?**

I have another upcoming book on spiritual warfare that will give you a lot more detail as to how to defend yourself, as a Christian, against satan who wants to steal, kill, and destroy all humans, whether they are saved or not. **Spiritual Warfare: How to armor up for a fight over your soul**

I am building an up-and-coming **world-wide website**, that by God's grace, will launch by the end of 2023 or early Spring of 2024. The website will have lots of Christians who live in your community for you to meet, videos to watch, many in-person activities with other Christians, and many worldwide online Bible studies in many different languages all around the world, and so much more. There is a lot to this new and exciting worldwide website, there are 15 different activities to do on this website which is what makes it so exciting. Once you see all that you can do on this website, it will make all other social and encouraging websites obsolete. Please keep me in prayer.

Please let me know if you want to be informed and updated on **the best Christian website ever!** Email me at: **TheBelieversGuide@yahoo.com**.

Thank you for reading this book and seeking a closer walk with God. I am consistently praying that this book will do what God has sent it to do **Isaiah 55:11** and that it touches hearts and changes lives.

May God Bless You and Keep You in His Hands.

Made in the USA
Middletown, DE
02 November 2025

19747336R00031